Original title:
The Glow of Green

Copyright © 2025 Creative Arts Management OÜ
All rights reserved.

Author: Mariana Leclair
ISBN HARDBACK: 978-1-80581-881-6
ISBN PAPERBACK: 978-1-80581-408-5
ISBN EBOOK: 978-1-80581-881-6

Spectral Garden Serenity

In a garden where fairies play,
The bushes dance in bright dismay.
Chasing shadows on the lawn,
Even gnomes are giggling on.

Moonlit Ferns

Under moonbeams, ferns take flight,
Skipping worms hold a dance tonight.
Crickets tune their best refrain,
While slugs plot to steal the fame.

Glints of Jade

Beetles sparkle like tiny spies,
They wear their colors with bold pride.
A grasshopper leaps with a wink,
Sipping dew like it's a drink!

Awakened Groves

Trees whisper secrets, oh so sly,
While birds crack jokes and then all fly.
Squirrels trade their nutty puns,
A chorus of laughs as the day runs.

Vibrant Echoes of Spring

In the garden, frogs wear hats,
As they leap, they chase the gnats.
The flowers giggle, colors bright,
A bee dressed up for a party night.

Squirrels dance, in a silly race,
Chasing each other, all over the place.
While daisies wave in a gentle breeze,
"Join us here!" they shout with ease.

The sunlight tricks the shadows long,
While crickets chirp a jazzy song.
A butterfly spilled paint in flight,
Creating chaos, what a sight!

Laughter echoes, the breeze is light,
Nature's jesters delight in the sight.
So join the fun, don't be late,
Spring's here to celebrate our fate!

Brilliance in the Underbrush

The hedgehogs wear their mother's shoes,
Making muddy paths, they share the views.
A rabbit slips on leafy mats,
Spinning faster, "No, not like that!"

The mushrooms chat with creeping vines,
Dodging raindrops, sipping wines.
They throw a feast, oh what delight,
"Come join us, it's a wild night!"

A snail slides slow, dreams of the race,
While a grasshopper hops with grace.
"Catch me if you can," he shouts with glee,
But the snail just laughs, "Not up to me!"

The ants are late, they lost their map,
Stumbling 'round in a goofy clap.
Amidst the leaves, let laughter flow,
In this green world, the fun will grow!

Ethereal Green Hues

In the forest, things dance and prance,
Where rabbits hold a fishing chance.
The trees wear dresses, swaying tall,
And whisper secrets, "We're on call!"

A lizard dons a tiny crown,
As bugs parade in the sun's renown.
"Let's have a ball!" the daisies shout,
While ants throw snacks, amidst the rout!

The wind joins in, with a playful spin,
Tickling leaves, and grinning wide within.
A chipmunk juggles seeds, oh dear,
While all applaud the carefree cheer.

Oh what a sight, in vibrant cheer,
Nature's laughter sings so clear.
Join the fun, don't miss the cue,
In this world of shades of hue!

Shimmering Moss Tales

On a log, a toad wears shades,
As he croaks, the sunlight fades.
A mossy patch whispers a joke,
"Join our club, come be our folk!"

The ladybugs play hide and seek,
Under leaves, they peek and squeak.
"Mossy slippers! It's my new trend!"
Said one with style that seems to bend.

The fallen acorns share tales bold,
Of nutty parties that never get old.
"Let's dance in circles," they decree,
While squirrels swing from the tallest tree.

So gather 'round this green delight,
In the woods where laughter is light.
For each tale spun, with giggles and sighs,
In the shimmer of green, joy truly lies!

Lush Luminance

In a forest where trees wear dresses of moss,
The squirrels throw parties, and no one feels cross.
A toad on a lily, with style so supreme,
Tells jokes to the crickets, sharing a dream.

The grass plays hide and seek, not a blade is still,
While bunnies join in, with a hop and a thrill.
An owl in a top hat, looking quite debonair,
Impresses the frogs with his dapper flair.

Mystical Greenery

Underneath ferns, a gnome starts to dance,
Chasing his hat that got caught in a trance.
A snail with a secret, he glides with such grace,
While telling the flowers they ought to keep pace.

The glow of bright leaves smiles down from above,
As bees serenade flowers, a buzz-laden love.
A frog with a banjo, strumming with glee,
Sings tunes to the beetles, a wild jubilee.

Emerald Reverie

A parrot with sunglasses lounges on a perch,
Claiming he knows where the funniest birds search.
The grasshoppers giggle, they leap in delight,
As worms in tuxedos hold a dance party night.

The leaves start to chatter, they gossip and sway,
With secrets of who took the last slice of bay.
A hedgehog in slippers joins in on the fun,
Declaring that softies are number one.

Ethereal Woodland Glow

There once was a fox with a very neat hat,
He hosted grand luncheons for friends—imagine that!
The mushrooms stood watch, all spruced up for the show,
With a twinkle and giggle, they put on a glow.

The fireflies practiced for their nightly parade,
Winking and blinking in a heavenly braid.
While rabbits served snacks, they couldn't quite keep,
Their noses twitching wildly, as they laughed in a heap.

Dappled Sunlight on Grass

In the meadow, squirrels dance,
Chasing shadows, take a chance.
Sunlight dapples, laughter rings,
Nature's play, oh, what it brings.

A butterfly, in polka dots,
Lands on flowers, ties its knots.
Ants are marching, all in line,
Swapping stories, oh, so fine.

The sun tickles blades, a jest,
Grasshoppers jumping, feeling blessed.
Chirping crickets crack a joke,
Even snails begin to poke.

A dog rolls in with gusto bright,
Muddy paws? It's a silly sight.
All around, a vibrant scene,
Where every creature wears a sheen.

Sparkling Thickets

In thickets dense, the critters prance,
Bouncing beams, they take a chance.
Hedgehogs giggle, chortle loud,
Tiny creatures feeling proud.

A raccoon dons a quirky hat,
Winks at birds, they have a spat.
Bushes buzz with whispers sweet,
Every leaf a secret treat.

Squirrels mock the sun above,
Throwing acorns, full of love.
Branches sway, a dance so merry,
While vines tickle, none are weary.

Beneath a hat of leafy green,
A party forms, oh, what a scene.
Nature's laugh, both wild and free,
In sparkles hidden, joy's decree.

Glistening Wilderness

In the wild, the laughter flows,
Glistening streams, where mischief grows.
A frog jumps in, a splash, a cheer,
Not quite graceful, but sincere.

Beneath the pines, the shadows play,
Foxes stumble, lost their way.
An owl hoots a chuckle wise,
As hedgehogs roll with silly sighs.

Mice are scampering, quick as light,
Dancing shadows in the night.
Stars above, they wink and tease,
While fireflies buzz, swaying with ease.

Berries dangle, oh so bright,
Gobbled down in pure delight.
In this realm of gleeful sights,
Nature's joy ignites the nights.

Vibrant Trails of Light

When trails of light paint the day,
Creatures join in a bright ballet.
Bouncing rabbits, what a sight,
Leaping high with all their might.

The sun peeks through the leafy dance,
A ladybug joins in the prance.
Chasing tails, they whisk away,
In this glowing, silly play.

A lizard strikes a pose and grins,
As flies parade, it slyly spins.
The path ahead, a radiant show,
Where giggles burst and wild things grow.

In every corner, laughter's thread,
While bees hum songs, no fear or dread.
With every step, the fun resumes,
In vibrant trails where joy resumes.

Celestial Greenery

In a field where the grass is tall,
A frog sings loud, what a hilarious call!
Worms dance like they're in a ballet,
While mushrooms giggle, what a funny play!

Fireflies twinkle in silly, bright hues,
As squirrels act out their best cartoon cues.
The wise old owl can't stop his laughter,
As bunnies hop faster, what's coming after?

Dandelions wink with a cheeky smile,
Chewing gum bubbles, they stretch a mile.
Even the trees shake, swaying with glee,
As nature's comedy unfolds for free!

So skip in the grass and dance with delight,
In this wacky world, everything feels right.
Where giggles abound and joy takes the stage,
Embrace the hilarity at every age!

Whirls of the Emerald Breeze

Up in the air, the leaves start to twirl,
As bugs crash in, making quite a whirl!
The wind blows gently, tickling my nose,
And the flowers chuckle, as humor grows!

Lizards lie back, playing 'king of the rock,'
While daisies, they giggle—oh what a shock!
The sun peeks in like it's on a spree,
Painting the scene in wild jubilee!

A snail takes a selfie, oh what a scene,
Instagram followers? The whole garden green!
With critters and plants, a party unfolds,
Every corner whispers a story bold!

So dance with the breeze, let laughter abound,
In fields of emerald where joy knows no bounds.
Every rustle and chuckle sings a sweet song,
In this vibrant haven, where we all belong!

Sprightly Green Reflections

In the pond, the lilies start to sway,
While frogs impersonate stars of the day!
Dragonflies zoom like they're on a race,
Bouncing on water with a funny grace!

The reeds join in, waving wildly around,
As fish tell jokes with a splashy sound.
"Why did the cat go to the green zone?"
"To see a fine plant that could make it groan!"

The turtles compete in their slow-motion chase,
While ants form a line, oh the silly pace!
"Jumping jacks!" yells a bug with crazy cheer,
As sunlight dances, making laughter clear!

With every bright hue and chuckle-filled view,
Life in the greens is refreshingly new.
So laugh with the critters, let joy take the lead,
In nature's own fairytale, let's all succeed!

Enveloped in Emerald Light

In a forest thick with laughter,
The trees play peek-a-boo,
Squirrels chuckle on their branches,
In a green-tinted view.

Frogs are croaking silly songs,
On lily pads afloat,
Even snails wear tiny hats,
As they begin to gloat.

A bear in shades of moss so bright,
Dances like it's grand,
While shadows sway in silly shapes,
In this funny land.

The sun begins to wink and shine,
Tickling every leaf,
A bouncing green parade unfolds,
And joy feels quite the chief.

Green Glimmer in Dusk

As twilight tiptoes shyly in,
The grass begins to glow,
Crickets join in on the fun,
With laughter in tow.

Fireflies flash like tiny stars,
Winking from the ground,
A beetle breaks into a jig,
In this giggle sound.

A rabbit slips and tumbles down,
Chasing after light,
While dandelion puffballs drift,
In a comical flight.

The evening wears a cloak of green,
With silliness and cheer,
In this whimsical realm we find,
Funny friends appear.

Dancing Light on Leaves

The sun spins tales on emerald leaves,
As breezes laugh and spin,
A squirrel sways in rhythmic beats,
With a cheeky little grin.

A chameleon does a funky dance,
In shades that change and play,
While ladybugs join for the fun,
In this wild ballet.

Raindrops tap and skip about,
Like they're in a race,
Even the roots seem to giggle,
In this vibrant space.

Nature laughs in shades of green,
With joy that's hard to beat,
Each twig and twig, a giggling kid,
Moving to the beat.

Kaleidoscope of Green

In a patchwork quilt of emerald hues,
The world does twist and turn,
A worm wears glasses, quite confused,
As the sun starts to burn.

Mossy rocks play hide and seek,
With giggling woodland sprites,
While chipmunks crack some corny jokes,
Under star-studded nights.

A dancing leaf flutters near,
As if it knows a tune,
While playful shadows spin and twirl,
Beneath the watchful moon.

In this kaleidoscope of fun,
With laughter all around,
Green grows wilder every day,
In this silly playground.

Shades of Radiant Life

In a forest, the wizards chat,
With squirrels dressed in tiny hats.
They brew up lots of weird green stew,
Claim it's healthy, but who knew?

The grass tickles all unhappy toes,
While frogs wear shades and strike cool poses.
The daisies dance, a sight to behold,
While bees share gossip, a tale retold.

Serene Verdancy

A turtle took a leap today,
Swam past the weeds like they were ballet.
He grinned as he zipped through the scene,
"Not bad for a shell, if you know what I mean!"

The trees wear coats of emerald hue,
And gossip trees whisper, "Oh, who knew?"
The leaves clap hands in a glorious jest,
While rabbits debate who's the fastest guest.

Glimmering Foliage

In a field of flowers wearing crowns,
The daisies giggle, turning frowns.
A sunflower takes a selfie with bees,
"I'm the star! Look at me, please!"

The bushes comment, "What a bright day!"
While the clumsy ants trip, in disarray.
With laughter that echoes through the trees,
Nature's humor floats on the breeze.

Nature's Luminous Embrace

A chameleon tries to fit in,
Changing shades, what a silly spin!
With each color swap, he cracks a smile,
"Just a fashionista, who's in the style!"

Worms gossip about the latest dirt,
While ladybugs boast of a new skirt.
The vivid hues dance with delight,
In nature's own cheerful, radiant light.

Illuminated Paths of Nature

In a forest where the critters dance,
Mossy stones take the chance to prance,
Frogs wear hats, quite the fashion show,
As squirrels juggle, putting on a glow.

Bright fireflies twinkle, a funny race,
Chasing shadows, oh what a chase!
Trees wear crowns made of green confetti,
While raccoons play cards, oh so petty.

Bees do the cha-cha, buzzing with cheer,
While owls hoot jokes, you can hear from here,
And hedgehogs roll in laughter's delight,
In the bright silliness of the night.

Each path leads to giggles, wild and free,
Where every leaf holds a mystery.
Let's dance with the critters, join in the fun,
In the glow of nature, our laughter's begun.

Emerald Whispers

In a meadow where the rabbits debate,
Green grass tickles as they all relate,
Whispers of daisies make giggly sounds,
While butterflies join in, flitting around.

A snail named Fred wore spectacles bright,
Claimed he was fast, but took all night,
As ladybugs titter, they flutter and tease,
Inviting more mischief, oh if you please.

The clouds overhead, fluffy and round,
Join in the laughter, a jovial sound,
As vines play hopscotch, swinging so high,
And frogs croak punchlines on the sly.

Emerald secrets dance on the breeze,
With every soft rustle, we're sure to seize,
The joyous tales spun in vibrant hues,
Where laughter blooms, and friendship ensues.

Luminous Ferns

In the glades where the ferns like to strut,
Critters roll by in a whimsical rut,
Bunnies tell stories of magical feats,
While chattering chipmunks tap dance on beats.

Luminous leaves with a wink in the light,
Invite all the hedgehogs for a party tonight,
Where ants juggle crumbs, oh what a sight,
And snails sing ballads of their epic flight.

The sun drops low, twinkling stars appear,
As trees crack a joke, making all cheer,
With laughter like raindrops, light and free,
We revel in nature's funny jubilee.

Let's skip through ferns where the silliness roams,
And find the joy in our vibrant homes,
For every green corner has laughter to lend,
In this happy embrace, all troubles suspend.

Radiance of the Forest

In the forest where sunlight takes a dive,
Trees wear sparkles, feel so alive,
Bears in sunglasses, lounging with style,
While parrots crack jokes, all the while.

Mushrooms giggle beneath their wide caps,
As porcupines map out hilarious laps,
Squirrels share gossip over acorn tea,
And moles work on puns, oh so crafty.

The brook, it chuckles, a bubbly tune,
Swaying willows dance under the moon,
With fireflies blinking, the party's aglow,
In a show of antics, laughter flows.

So let us all gather, join in the jest,
In the forest's embrace, we feel truly blessed,
With nature's bright comedy, clever and keen,
Every moment sparkles, a joyous sheen.

Emerald Whispers

In a forest where frogs sing,
Mossy hats in a funky bling.
Chasing shadows that jump and dance,
Squirrels plotting their nutty prance.

A turtle in shades, moving slow,
Complaints of the sun's bright show.
The rabbits hop in a silly race,
Each one trying to win first place.

Breezes tickle each leaf's tip,
As ants hold a wild, dance party trip.
The toads croak jokes with a croaky cheer,
"Best place for laughs? Come hop over here!"

At dusk, the fireflies twinkle and tease,
They giggle around, doing as they please.
The night wears its sparkly crown,
In this silly, emerald gown.

Luminous Forest Dreams

In the woods where shadows play,
Bunnies mingle in their way.
With carrots held in tiny paws,
They throw parties for all the flaws.

A raccoon dons a shiny hat,
Sipping juice from a forest vat.
He tells tall tales of his great heist,
"How I stole that cake — oh, what a feast!"

The trees shake their leaves in good cheer,
As chipmunks crack up, "Is that deer here?"
Each twig and branch joins in the fun,
Under the rays of a setting sun.

The moon peeks through with a wink so sly,
"Keep laughing, folks, don't let it die!"
In dreams of green, the mischief flows,
With the friends we've made, anything goes.

Radiance Among the Leaves

Underneath a canopy bright,
Bugs boogie till the end of night.
With disco moves on leafy floors,
They twirl and spin by nature's doors.

A dandy deer with big ol' shoes,
Steps to a beat, oh what a muse!
He takes a leap with a comical flair,
Before tripping over a vine, unaware.

In this splendid space of vibrant play,
Mice wear sunglasses, enjoying the day.
A quirky scene of giggles and grins,
As they join in the fun while the party spins.

Even the butterflies join the fête,
With graceful flutters and moves so great.
In this wild garden, the spirits soar,
With laughter echoing forevermore.

Verdant Light

In a meadow with patchy grass,
A frog leaps high, "Watch me, with class!"
He plops in the pond, creating a splash,
While fireflies laugh, with a little dash.

A lizard in shades sips lemonade,
A lazy cucumber parade displayed.
He claims he's the coolest of the crew,
"Who knew green could be so cool too?"

The hedgehogs roll in a leafy race,
Spinning around in their fluffy lace.
"Hold onto your hats, it's a crazy ride!"
As leaves rustle, they grip and glide.

With chirps and giggles wrapping the night,
Creatures bask in this silly light.
In their green kingdom, all is bright,
As fun and laughter take flight.

Safire and Emerald Streams

In the creek where frogs convene,
Jumping jokes they share unseen.
With splashes bright and laughter wide,
They hold a party, no need to hide.

Fish in scales of greenish hue,
Wiggle and dance, it's quite the view!
They've got moves that would make you grin,
Splashing water and spinning fins.

A turtle joins, with a slow, sly smirk,
Claims to teach the fish some work.
But all he did was take a nap,
Dreaming sweet, on a sunny lap.

At twilight's kiss, they bid adieu,
Echoes of giggles fade from view.
Under stars, creek bubbles sway,
Fun in green, till light of day!

Glowing Moss

In the forest where the mossy bits,
Lies a party of tiny crits.
With mushrooms dressed in polka dots,
They jiggle and wiggle in funny spots.

A squirrel claims the dance floor's throne,
On a log that's all his own.
He spins and twirls with a nut in hand,
The audience cheers, it's quite the stand!

A bunny hops in with a funky hat,
With twinkly shoes and a bird as chat.
But when he jumps, he takes a dive,
Rolling in moss, oh what a vibe!

As dusk falls down with fairy lights,
The critters laugh through starry nights.
In this green world of giggly bliss,
They dance and play, it's pure happiness!

Chlorophyll Symphony

In the canopy where leaves sway,
Nature holds a concert today.
Crickets strum their tiny strings,
While squirrels trumpet with funny flings.

Bees join in with a buzzing sound,
As they waltz 'round with leaps profound.
The ants march in, a line so neat,
With tiny boots that tap to the beat!

A caterpillar starts a slow dance,
Wiggling his way to win a chance.
But slips and rolls, oh what a sight,
He laughs it off, 'I'll fly in flight!'

The nightingale sings a silly tune,
Under the light of a bright green moon.
In this symphony of nature's cheer,
Even the trees sway without fear!

Glimmering Underbrush

In the thicket where shadows play,
The critters plan a grand ballet.
With twinkling fireflies forming lines,
They wiggle and giggle like silly pines.

A hedgehog prances, all spines aglow,
Claiming he leads the dazzling show.
But trips on leaves, oh what a fall,
Rolling down, he bounces, and all!

A chipmunk shimmies with nuts to share,
Balancing treats without a care.
Yet in a twist, he drops the stash,
A nutty joke turned into a crash!

As moonlight beams on this silly scene,
The underbrush sparkles, truly keen.
With laughter echoing all around,
In nature's glow, fun can be found!

Reflections of Chlorophyll

In the forest where light plays,
Leaves dance their silly ballet.
Lizards wearing shades of lime,
Giggle and bask, oh what a time!

Frogs croak jokes with croaky tones,
Mossy benches, our green throne.
Squirrels with acorns run amok,
It's hard to find a grumpy rock!

Sunlight sips the dew like wine,
As ants march in a single line.
Oh, nature laughs with every jest,
In this green realm, we're truly blessed!

So come on friends, let's take a stroll,
Where every leaf's a comic roll.
In laugh and shush, we leap and bound,
In this verdant playland we have found.

Luminescent Treetops

Amidst the branches, shine and gleam,
The birds are plotting their next scheme.
A parrot parodies the moon,
While raccoons dance to a catchy tune!

Fireflies swing in disco lights,
While owls wear wigs and funny tights.
Trees chuckle in the evening haze,
Sharing jokes in their leafy maze.

Bamboo bends with glee at night,
Tickled by the stars so bright.
They whisper secrets, oh so sly,
While winds howl their silly sigh.

So gather round, let's hear the tale,
Of leafy laughter that cannot fail.
In the treetops up above,
Nature's humor is what we love!

Mystic Grove's Embrace

In a grove where giggles sprout,
Benches pop up, they're all about.
Trees bend down for a friendly hug,
While tiny bugs play tug-of-war with a rug!

Mushrooms grin with wobbly glee,
Toadstools tap dance, wild and free.
A hedgehog spinning on a dime,
Makes everyone laugh, oh what a rhyme!

Whispering winds with a cheeky flair,
Sneeze the leaves into the air.
In this nook of cheer and fun,
Nature's mischief has just begun!

So take a seat, enjoy the show,
Where every creature steals the glow.
In this embrace so snug and tight,
Laughter echoes through the night.

Glittering Green Fauna

A grasshopper sings with a wobbly tune,
While slugs wear shells like a cartoon.
Beetles strut in glittery gear,
In this wild jungle of snorts and cheer!

Caterpillars argue who's the best,
While ladybugs play a game of chess.
Crickets chirp with punchy flair,
As dragonflies zoom through the air.

Frogs joke about their candid fame,
Claiming they can change their name!
Toads chuckle, "You'll never be a star,"
As they hop around with a wink and spar.

So join the party in the lush terrain,
Where every creature has something to gain.
Here amidst laughter and silly pranks,
We find joy in all the green flanks!

Silhouettes of Sage

In a garden where veggies dance,
Chubby cucumbers prance in a trance.
Radishes wear hats like dapper gents,
While the chives plot pranks with mischievous intents.

Basil thinks he's a movie star,
Dreams of a career that'll take him far.
Peppers giggle, hiding in the patch,
As they try on costumes, a colorful match.

Mirth in the Mushrooms

In damp woodlands where fungi spread,
Mushrooms giggle, gossiping instead.
One wore a crown, feeling quite grand,
While others danced to a band made of sand.

Toadstools tell tales of the tallest trees,
How they once swayed in the springtime breeze.
Chanting their songs beneath the moonlight,
With each little cap, they shared pure delight.

Light's Glistening Tapestry

Lime-colored light spills from the sky,
While sprightly fairies in twirls pass by.
They paint the flowers with polka dots,
Laughing so hard, they forget their plots.

Willows sway like they're in a show,
With branches that wink and leaves that glow.
The daisies join in a lyrical rhyme,
As the sun tickles them, 'Oh, it's playtime!'

Rejuvenating Green Light

Spinach dreams of being a star,
While kale's off chasing snacks from afar.
Lettuce tasks the peas with a mission,
To start the day with a salad rendition.

As broccoli flexes those floral fists,
Zucchini juggles, waving, 'I exist!'
An avocado slides down the vine,
With guacamole jokes, tasty and fine.

Shining Wildflowers

In the meadow, flowers prank,
Dressed in hues, they laugh and thank.
Bee in bowtie, what a sight,
Buzzing jokes, day turns bright.

Dandelions pull a stunt,
Windswept hats, they lead the hunt.
Tulips chuckle, petals sway,
Tickled by the sun's warm play.

A daisy shouts, 'I'm not plain!',
While violets boast of their reign.
Petal petals, come and see,
Nature's jesters, live and free!

In this court of colors bold,
Each bloom a tale, a laugh retold.
Join the dance, don't be shy,
With wildflowers, you'll surely fly!

Summer's Emerald Embrace

A leafy hat upon your head,
Sipping lemonade, while you wed.
The trees whispering, oh so sly,
'Let's have a picnic!' they say, 'Oh my!'

Grass tickles toes, a soft delight,
Skateboarding ants in sheer sunlight.
The squirrels debate who brings the nuts,
While sunlight decorates their huts.

Giggling leaves begin to dance,
With a breeze that gives them a chance.
'You missed a spot!' one leaf cries,
As sunlight paints their leafy ties.

In this embrace, laughter thrives,
Each moment, a joy, alive!
Savor the chaos, feel the cheer,
Nature's fun parade is here!

Illumined Trellises

Climbing vines in a tricky race,
Reaching up, a leafy chase.
Each tendril stretches, giving a show,
'Watch me grow!' they gleefully crow.

Grapevines wrangle, 'Don't you dare,
Stay behind, I'm light as air!'
With blooms like jester hats atop,
They giggle at the garden shop.

Bumblebees wear tiny caps,
Sipping nectar, blissful laps.
'Another round!' they hum in jest,
While roses blush, 'We're the best!'

Sunset paints a vibrant scene,
Cheerful hues, a vivid dream.
In this arboreal delight,
Whimsical heartbeats twinkle bright!

Foliage in Flicker

Leaves swing low, a quirky crew,
Wiggling hips, they dance anew.
'Watch this twist!' a branch will tease,
As shadows pirouette with ease.

Mischief managed in the glade,
As tease the ferns with antics played.
'Catch me if you can,' they laugh,
The oaks shake heads, 'Do the math!'

A squirrel performs the latest trend,
While acorns roll, they do not bend.
'Ouch! My hat!' a leaf did cry,
As breezes giggle, oh so spry.

In nature's laugh, we find our cheer,
Each flicker brightens, drawing near.
Join the foliage in this spree,
Where joy is free, just wait and see!

Verdant Dreams

In a land where the broccoli blooms,
And the spinach sings funny tunes,
Kale does a jig, peas pop in glee,
Cauliflower joins in a green jubilee.

Grass blades giggle under the sun,
While moss takes naps, all cozy and fun,
A pickled cucumber tries to dance,
But ends up stuck in a vegetable trance.

Lettuce rollers at the garden's edge,
Spinach longboards on a leafy ledge,
Radishes chuckle as they sprout,
"I swear I'm the best vegetable!" they shout.

In this bouncy green wonderland,
Where every plant dances as it can,
A humorously bright, leafy spectacle,
Nature's own wacky, herbal carnival.

Glistening Canopies

Underneath that leafy dome,
Where butterflies giggle, feeling at home,
The sunlight sparkles, makes them twirl,
As the ferns giggle and the wildflowers whirl.

A squirrel puts on a shiny new tie,
As the birds crack jokes, soon to reply,
"I can't believe how bright it is!"
Squeaks the shy squirrel with a chortle and fizz.

Mushrooms pop up, acting all bold,
While sunbeams tickle, shining like gold,
"Did you hear the one about the leaf?"
The branches laugh, oh what a relief!

A cacophony of chuckles, a leafy affair,
Nature's own jokes float into the air,
In this bouncy kaleidoscope up high,
Laughter in the branches, oh my, oh my!

Celestial Jade

In the park where jade turtles lie,
They trade jokes, oh my, oh my!
One told of the moon, round and bright,
Who thought it could dance but missed its flight.

Starlight giggles through branches galore,
As nightshade whispers, "I'm not a bore!"
The dewdrops chuckle, glisten and tease,
"Careful, don't slip on these slippery leaves!"

Winkling stars, a wobbly team,
Play hide and seek in a leafy dream,
With laughter that rustles those emerald coats,
In a game of jokes where everyone gloats.

So here's to the night in celestial glee,
Where laughter erupts among foliage free,
A wacky wonderland under the skies,
As nature jokes and twinkles, oh my, what a surprise!

Illumination of Leaves

In a forest where leaves flirt and play,
With shadows that dance in a quirky ballet,
The sunlight tickles the branches tall,
And the laughter echoes, oh how it calls.

"Did you hear about the green apple's dream?"
Asked the banana, who glimmered and gleamed,
"It wanted to be a shining star,
Instead, it rolled down the hill too far!"

A monkey swings with a bright green hat,
While chattering squirrels discuss this and that,
"Oh, to be a leaf, swirling and free,
Just floating on laughter, who wouldn't agree?"

With each giggle, the leaves brightly beam,
Sharing the joy, as if in a dream,
A dizzying dance, all nature receives,
In this whimsical world of illuminating leaves.

Verdant Lightplay

In the forest, leaves do dance,
Wobbling like a pants-wearing prance.
Squirrels in shades, looking quite snazzy,
Chasing each other, getting rather jazzy.

Mossy carpets that tickle your toes,
And bugs in tuxes strike silly poses.
A frog on a log croaks like a king,
Each note a giggle, what a funny thing!

When sunlight winks, the ferns all gleam,
Grass stains appear, like a child's dream.
Nature's comedy club, full of cheer,
Who knew that green could tickle the ear?

So pull up a seat, join in the fun,
The leafy laughter has just begun.
With sprouts that impress and chuckles abound,
This playful greenery dances around!

Whispering Green Shadows

Under the boughs, shadows play peek,
Making the mushrooms giggle and squeak.
A rabbit in shades, sipping his tea,
Cracks jokes to birds, 'Why fly when you can bee?'

The green grass whispers, 'I'm ticklish!'
While ants in a row act all regal and swish.
Chasing the sun, the daisies all sway,
'We're in a dance-off!' they seem to say.

In the depths of the ferns, a prankster awaits,
A turtle who thinks he can dance with the mates.
With a wiggle and jiggle, he steals the show,
But slips on a leaf, oh no, off he goes!

The wind tells tales, with a giggle or two,
As leaves rustle softly, sharing the view.
In the shady green corner, laughter abounds,
With whispers of humor where joy can be found!

Nature's Luminescent Veil

A quirky leaf draped in morning light,
Rubbing its eyes, 'Am I quite alright?'
It stumbles on branches, then gives a cheer,
'Look, I'm a disco ball, have no fear!'

The daisies chuckle, with petals so bright,
Swaying to rhythms that feel just right.
Caterpillars twist in a tango of glee,
Worms take a bow, 'We're all joined at sea!'

With bushes that giggle and grasses that grin,
A jolly old fox sneaks in for a spin.
It trips on a vine, then rolls in the muck,
And all of the critters shout, 'What's up, dud-duc?'

Then come the fireflies, bustling about,
Winking their lights, 'We know what it's about!'
They sparkle and tease, in a whimsical race,
The punchline of nature with laughter's embrace!

Sparkling Green Canvases

Dancing in sunlight, the grass wears a smile,
While vines twist and twirl, going wild all the while.
Each leaf is a brush stroke in artistry green,
Creating a canvas both bright and serene.

Trees with their branches stretch out like a hand,
Telling bold stories of the great leafy land.
A chipmunk, a jester, with acorns to toss,
Dances on the stage without a sense of gloss.

Skimming the surface, the brook bubbles fast,
With bubbles popping jokes, so there's no need to last.
Each splash of water laughs at the rocks,
While frogs play hopscotch, they've lost all their socks!

In meadows so vivid, paint splashes all night,
With hues of hilarious etched into sight.
So let's wander freely, where joy does abound,
In nature's own story where laughter is found!

Enchanted Emeralds

In a forest of mischief, they play,
Little sprites dance on leaves all day.
With hiccuping laughter, they twirl around,
Sprinkling giggles upon the ground.

A frog in a top hat jumps quite high,
Chasing butterflies that zoom by.
He trips on a root, oh what a sight,
Turns a tumble into pure delight.

Mossy carpets welcome each step,
Squirrel acrobats take their prep.
They flip and twirl, can't stay still,
Chasing their tails over the hill.

Shimmering shadows skip and hop,
Playing tag 'til they drop.
With smiles so wide, they part the trees,
Tickling the air with gentle tease.

Evergreen Resonance

A parrot perched with a comic flair,
Tells jokes to squirrels, who giggle and stare.
His feathers shine in the morning sun,
As he cracks puns, oh it's so much fun!

The rabbits boast of speed so grand,
But trip on grass, can't make a stand.
With wiggly tails and floppy ears,
They bounce back up amidst their cheers.

A wise old owl with glasses so round,
Reads fortunes from the lost and found.
He chuckles softly, gives a wink,
"Life's too short, just grab a drink!"

In this green realm, where laughter reigns,
All of nature plays its funny games.
With every rustle and cheerful squeak,
A world of jesters, so unique!

Vibrant Hues of Nature

The daisies wear hats, oh what a sight,
Pansies throw parties each springtime night.
Butterflies gossip, sharing a laugh,
While daisies argue about their half.

A hedgehog painted bright, is on the run,
Rolling in colors, just having fun.
He bumps into flowers, sends seeds a-flying,
Twirling and tumbling, no sign of crying.

Ladybugs laugh at their polka dot woes,
As they dance on the tips of garden hose.
They spin and swirl, a jovial crew,
With petals and pollen, a vibrant view.

All around, nature's rib-tickling show,
With snickers and snorts that freely flow.
In every glade, a ticklish breeze,
Ticking off time while they tease!

Dappled Light in the Woods

Sunlight spots dance on forest floors,
Where chipmunks plan their playful wars.
In a dappled court, they duel with glee,
Using acorns as their weaponry.

A bear with a hat and shoes too tight,
Tries to fly kites but takes off in fright.
He stumbles and fumbles, oh what a case,
Rolling downhill, he's lost in space!

The trees applaud his silly descent,
Echoes of laughter become their intent.
The brook chuckles, spilling jokes so fast,
While shadows giggle, their shadows cast.

In this woodland realm, fun's never shy,
With every twirl and each silly high.
The leaves rustle lyrics, the branches sway,
As nature's clowns join in the play!

Celestial Green Dance

In a froggy tutu, they prance,
With leaps and bounds, they take their chance.
The crickets chirp a jazzy tune,
While fireflies groove beneath the moon.

Swaying leaves join the party too,
A vine slips on its brand new shoe.
The branches swing in merry glee,
Who knew the woods held such a spree!

The snails bring chips, the worms play bass,
While mushrooms glow, setting the pace.
The night unfolds, the fun won't cease,
As nature bounces, all at peace.

The stars peek down, they can't resist,
Joining in this leafy twist.
They twirl among the roots so spry,
In this dance floor, oh me, oh my!

Lush Radiance

A cactus dons a sparkling crown,
While grasshoppers spin around town.
The daisies wear their polka dots,
Kooky antics, connecting the dots.

The thistles throw a wild bash,
As bumblebees join in a splash.
The gardener busts out his guitar,
So everyone sings, 'Hey, how bizarre!'

Tall trees sway with a goofy grin,
While squirrels chuck acorns in.
With laughter bubble and songs so sweet,
The garden's dance is quite the feat.

A sunbeam bounces off the pond,
Creating ripples that go beyond.
As silly shadows start to prance,
Nature laughs, and takes a chance!

The Brightness Beneath the Canopy

Beneath the leaves, a party brews,
Frogs in shades of neon hues.
The woodpecker takes the mic to sing,
While ladybugs get ready to swing.

The caterpillars make a line,
In a conga, looking so divine.
A hippo tried to join this spree,
But tripped and fell; oh, what a sight to see!

With mushrooms serving cupcakes bright,
And ants setting up for a cake fight.
The forest floor is filled with cheer,
As critters laugh, no holding back fear.

In this lively, leafy retreat,
Nature's jesters can't be beat.
The laughter echoes, crisp and pure,
Fun in the shade, that's for sure!

Twinkling Fern Worlds

Under ferns, secrets start to bloom,
As paragraphs of laughter fill the room.
Mice wear hats, as bold as gold,
Pondering tales from days of old.

The pixies play a game of tag,
With flying pistachios in a bag.
A sneaky squire's up to no good,
Trying to steal nuts, as squirrels brood.

The tadpoles chat about their dreams,
To hop and dive in sunlit streams.
A dragonfly brings lemonade jerk,
While critters sip, and giggles lurk.

As shadows dance with limbs so spry,
The fun beneath the greenery won't die.
The world of ferns, alive and bright,
Bound in humor, pure delight!

Light-Dripped Petals

In a garden where lettuce wears suits,
The peas tell jokes under leafy boots.
Carrots giggle, sprouting up high,
While radishes blush, oh my, oh my!

Each herb is a critic, with witty flair,
Chives whisper gossip, light as air.
The potatoes roll their eyes in dismay,
"Why's everyone laughing? It's just the way!"

Cabbages dance in a froggy beat,
Beets are the drummers with rhythm so sweet.
Tomatoes chuckle, ripe and round,
In this silly patch, joy knows no bound!

Nature's playground, a quirky bout,
Flowers in laughter, what's that about?
Under the sun, they wobbly prance,
In this whimsy world, come join the dance!

Twilight in Verdant Valleys

In valleys where critters wear hats so tall,
The squirrels debate who has the best haul.
The grass stands up, all prim and neat,
While crickets compete with tap-dancing feet.

Fireflies twinkle like stars on a dare,
Making a scene of aerial flair.
A hedgehog cracks jokes in his prickly style,
While the owl hoots, "Just stay for a while!"

Bunny in shades sipping clover tea,
Whispers to badgers, "Just let it be!"
The evening brings giggles from under the trees,
As nature holds court, full of quirk and ease.

So raise a glass of dew, let's toast the night,
To valleys in laughter, oh what a sight!
Under the moon that's grinning with cheer,
All creatures unite; it's the best time of year!

Bioluminescent Blooms

In a forest where mushrooms wear neon hues,
Dancing in jigs to the gnomes' little blues.
The daisies are blushing, glowing away,
"We're the disco flowers! Join us, okay?"

Each petal's a lantern, each leaf's a thrill,
Under starlit skies, with laughter to spill.
The ferns chuckle softly, rustling their leaves,
With winks from the willows that nobody believes.

Glow worms are poets, their words come alive,
Reciting sweet verses to fireflies five.
"Oh light up your life!" says the elder oak,
As critters lose track of the funny they poke.

So sway and twirl in phosphorescent delight,
For nature's a stage, and it's quite a sight.
Join in the merriment, don't be shy,
In this glowing realm, we'll dance until we fly!

Radiant Nature's Palette

On canvas of Earth, colors swirl and twine,
With daisies like artists, painting the vine.
Poppies in red are bold and bright,
While sunflowers draw smiles, oh what a sight!

The lilacs giggle, in gentle lilac sways,
"Who wears it best?" in their blooming displays.
While violets smirk, tucked in corners so sly,
Saying, "Watch out! Here comes the butterfly!"

Marigolds gossip in sunny delight,
As blooms poke fun at the nearby bulb's height.
"Stand up, dear tulip! It's your time to shine,
Get that head up high, sip nectar and wine!"

In nature's bright palette, we sway to the tune,
With laughter that echoes, a melodious boon.
So join in the fun, let colors collide,
In this radiant world, let happiness abide!

SunlitParterre

In the garden, critters dance,
Sunflowers wear their golden pants.
Bees play hide and seek with cheer,
While ants march off without a fear.

Lettuce giggles, sprouts attest,
To tales of veggies on a quest.
Tomatoes blush with ripened pride,
As radishes chuckle, side by side.

Butterflies wear their wings with glee,
Whispering secrets to the bee.
The soil tickles roots below,
As veggies flaunt their vibrant show.

Forests of Elven Light

In forests where the fairies tease,
Trees wear hats made of the leaves.
Squirrels scurry with acorn dreams,
While sunlight giggles through the beams.

Mushrooms gather for a feast,
With woodland critters as their guests.
They toast with dew and laugh till night,
In the shadows, creatures take flight.

Rabbits hop with joyful flair,
While hedgehogs take the cushy chair.
The brook hums tunes, a giddy song,
As nightfall comes; they dance along.

Iridescent Herbals

Herbs in pots have quite the sass,
Mint quips jokes while basil laughs.
Rosemary, in a chef's tall hat,
Sways along with thyme, a witty brat.

Chives whisper secrets in the shade,
Parsley's pose is quite well played.
Oregano's mischief fills the air,
While cilantro does a dapper hair.

Tom and Pepper form a duo bold,
With stories of seasonings retold.
In the kitchen, they will prance,
As spices join the dinner dance.

Beacons in the Wilderness

In wilds where the critters sing,
Fireflies bling like tiny kings.
The moon winks at a cheeky bat,
While raccoons plan a midnight chat.

Bears in the berries chuckle loud,
As elk strut past, feeling proud.
A crickets' band kicks off the show,
As owls hoot in sleepy flow.

The foxes craft their shifty scheme,
Plotting pranks like a wild dream.
Nature's light, a playful gleam,
In wilderness, it's all a meme.

Nature's Verdant Glow

In a field of lettuce, a rabbit took flight,
Chasing a carrot, he danced with delight.
A squirrel in shades, so dapper and spry,
Wore a leaf as a hat, oh my, oh my!

The daisies were giggling, their petals all bright,
While worms in the soil planned a wild karaoke night.
A frog on a lily pad croaked a soft tune,
Dreaming of snacks beneath the big moon.

The grass blades were swaying, a verdant ballet,
Tickling the toes of the deer on their way.
But one sneaky snail, with a wink and a grin,
Slid into the party, not wanting to miss in!

As the sun dipped low, colors danced in a swirl,
Chasing the shadows, the crickets would twirl.
In nature's great theatre, the laughter would flow,
Celebrating joys in a green, giggly glow!

Emerald Enchantment

A pickle parade danced down the lane,
Wobbling and jiggling, causing a strain.
For the cucumbers laughed, 'We're in a big show!'
As they twirled and they twisted, all friendly like, yo!

The kale leaves were gossiping, trading their flair,
About a bold avocado who tried to fly fair.
An onion piped up, with a wink and a gruff,
'Just don't cry now, this green is enough!'

An elf in a glade sat on mushrooms so round,
Wishing for chips, the best snack he had found.
With a guacamole dip, he planned the delight,
In emerald skies, munching under the night!

The ferns whispered secrets where no one could hear,
As they jived with the breeze, spreading plenty of cheer.
So in this strange realm where the green takes a lead,
Laughter follows closely, planting joy like a seed!

Shimmering Grasslands

In the shimmering fields where the wildflowers sway,
A clan of cheeky gophers came out to play.
They wore tiny boots made of dewy green grass,
Trying to dance but were tripping, alas!

A parrot above squawked with vibrant delight,
'Join my karaoke with voices so bright!'
But the turtles were slow, taking their time,
Singing off-key, but they felt it was prime.

Bunnies with shades played hopscotch on clover,
With a scoreboard of chips, not a single four-leafed cover.

While a hedgehog juggled ripe berries with flair,
Declaring, 'I'm the king! You know, if you care!'

As the sun set down, the glow began to rise,
The laughter erupted, they reached for the skies.
In these grasslands of joy, where the green spirits beam,
Life's a funny dance, like a whimsical dream!

Radiant Canopy

Underneath the leaves where the sunlight plays,
A monkey proclaimed, 'I'm the king of this maze!'
With a hat made of twigs and a grin so wide,
He swung from the branches, full of mischief and pride.

The owls were hooting, planning a scheme,
To throw a wild party, a nocturnal dream.
They wore capes of moss and had popcorn to pop,
Inviting the critters, 'Now, don't you dare stop!'

The raccoons all gathered, with masks on their face,
Ready for fun in their leafy hide place.
Whilst sharing their snacks, a big slip happened,
With a tumble of leaves, oh, the laughter just crackled!

As the stars twinkled down, a wonderful scene,
The creatures all danced in their marvelous green.
For in this high canopy, silliness blooms,
While joy resonates deep from the roots to the rooms!

www.ingramcontent.com/pod-product-compliance
Lightning Source LLC
Chambersburg PA
CBHW070329120526
44590CB00017B/2842